Unknown
Unknown

BOOKSHOPS AND
THE DELIGHT OF
NOT GETTING WHAT
YOU WANTED

MARK FORSYTH

ICON

Published in the UK in 2014 by
Icon Books Ltd, Omnibus Business Centre,
39–41 North Road, London N7 9DP
email: info@iconbooks.com
www.iconbooks.com

Sold in the UK, Europe, South Africa and Asia
by Faber & Faber Ltd, Bloomsbury House,
74–77 Great Russell Street,
London WC1B 3DA or their agents

Distributed in the UK, Europe and Asia
by TBS Ltd, TBS Distribution Centre, Colchester Road,
Frating Green, Colchester CO7 7DW

Distributed in South Africa
by Jonathan Ball, Office B4, The District,
41 Sir Lowry Road, Woodstock 7925

Distributed in Australia and New Zealand
by Allen & Unwin Pty Ltd,
PO Box 8500, 83 Alexander Street,
Crows Nest, NSW 2065

ISBN: 978-184831-784-0

Typeset in Minion by Marie Doherty

Printed and bound in the UK by Clays Ltd, St Ives plc

To Julia Kingsford

(Because I'm too frightened not to)

About the author

MARK FORSYTH is a writer whose books have made him one of the UK's best-known commentators on words and the English language. His most recent book, *The Elements of Eloquence*, told the story of the flowers of rhetoric. *The Etymologicon* was a *Sunday Times* #1 bestseller and BBC Radio 4 'Book of the Week', as was his second book *The Horologicon*. He writes the Inky Fool blog and has contributed articles to the *Guardian*, *Daily Telegraph*, *Spectator*, *New York Times* and *Wall Street Journal* among others. He lives in Clerkenwell, London.

The Unknown Unknown

Most of my opinions on bookshops were formed by Donald Rumsfeld. In case you've forgotten, or never knew, Donald Rumsfeld was the American Secretary of Defense in the administrations of both Gerald Ford and the younger Mr Bush. He is often rather hysterically accused of starting unnecessary wars, believing he is above International Law, and being more interested in origami than in human life; but that is not all that he and I have in common. It's his opinion on the necessity of bookshops that truly binds us together.

> There are things we know that we know. There are known unknowns. That is to say there are things that we now know we don't know. But there are also unknown unknowns. There are things we do not know we don't know.

For some reason that I shall never understand, there are those who find these lines perplexing. They ridicule it. The Plain English Campaign even awarded Mr Rumsfeld their

Foot in Mouth Award of 2003 for 'a baffling comment by a public figure'. But there's nothing baffling in it really. I know that Paris is the capital of France, but more importantly *I know* that I know Paris is the capital of France. I know that I don't know the capital of Azerbaijan, although I'm sure that they have one. It's the sort of thing I really ought to check up on. But I do not know … well, here it gets complicated. You do not know that you do not know the capital of Erewhon, because you had no idea that there was a country called Erewhon, and therefore you had no idea that there was a gap in your knowledge. You did not know that you did not know.

The same thing applies to books. I know that I've read *Great Expectations*: it is a known known. I know that I haven't read *War and Peace*: it is a known unknown to me (and barring a long prison sentence is likely to remain so). But there are also books that I've never heard of; and, because I've never heard of them, I've no idea that I haven't read them.

I'd love to name one of these books that I haven't heard of. I'd love to give you examples, but, you see, I can't because I've never heard of them. Tolstoy, Stendhal and Cervantes, these men follow me around. They stand in dark corners and eye me disapprovingly from beneath supercilious eyebrows. And all because I've never got round to reading their blasted, thousand-page, three-ton, five-generation, state-of-a-nation thingummywhatsits. I don't care. Or rather, sometimes I do, and at other times I remember that I'm a tortoise-slow reader and that there's a pub just around the corner. Testes to Tolstoy, that's what I say; and I say it in full knowledge of his vast reputation and beard.

But the others. Where are they? Who are they? I've absolutely no idea. They're probably having a party next door. The best sort of party filled with beautiful wines and delicious women. But I am not invited. Not that I can blame them. We've never met. And I can't find them, because I don't know their names. They are the unknown unknown, and I can't even pine after them, such is my double ignorance.

And thus and therefore the bookshop; for, though there is a popular myth that Mr Rumsfeld was discussing Mesopotamian weaponry, he was, of course, discussing methods of buying books. We are all a little misunderstood at times.

There are, as he said, three kinds of books: the ones you've read, the ones you know you haven't read (like *War and Peace*), and the others: the books you don't know you don't know.

The ones you've read, you don't need to buy. Presumably, you bought (or at least filched) a copy before reading. The famous books that you haven't read – the known unknowns – are easily obtainable: they are on the internet. You type in *War and Peace* and all sorts of book-traders mention that they have it available for tuppence ha'penny, and that a nice young man will bring it to your door by tea time.

I believe that here I ought to bemoan the modern age and go on about how human contact is lost and we're all going to Hell on a handcart, but I just can't. The internet is much too convenient. Perhaps life was a lot healthier in the days when everything was done in person. But it was much more time-consuming as well. Also, you can carry on this line of false nostalgia for ever. People hated paperbacks when they came in, and referred to them as *penny dreadfuls*. And I suspect that when Johannes Gutenberg invented the printing press in the 15th century, the monasteries were filled with monks saying that a *printed* Bible lacked the human touch. You can probably go all the way back to 3000 BC and find an Egyptian complaining that hieroglyphics were being pushed out by the new-fangled hieratic script. It never ends.

The world has moved on and all sorts of things have gone into the darkness – steam engines, cassette tapes and smallpox. Shriek as we might, we don't truly want them back. The internet is a splendid invention, and it won't go away. If you know you want something, the internet can get it for you. My point, and the whole point of this essay, is that it's not enough to get what you already know you wanted. The best things are the things you never knew you wanted until you got them.

The internet takes your desires and spits them back out at you, consummated. You search, you put in the words you know, the things that were already on your mind, and it gives you back a book or a picture or a Wikipedia article. But that is all. The unknown unknown must be found otherwise.

STRANGE BOOKS

I am the proud possessor of a strange literary rarity: *Fiction First: An anthology of short stories written by the employees of First UK Bus*. It's actually remarkably good, and I've never felt comfortable on a First UK bus since, as I see all other authors as potential threats. But you, dear reader, cannot buy this book. You will never own a copy because, as it says on the back, it is NOT FOR GENERAL SALE. The only reason I have a copy is that, like most of the nobler things in life, somebody had simply abandoned it in the changing area at the swimming ponds on Hampstead Heath, where I found it one April afternoon.

And if I hadn't found it lying there on a bench, I would never have known that I hadn't found it.

Such serendipities are rare. They occur occasionally in guest bedrooms and other people's lavatories. Did you know that there is a book entirely devoted to photographs of old lavatories in the Cotswolds? Nor did I, until I stayed in that hotel in Cheltenham.[1]

I discovered the works of Bohumil Hrabal under a friend's sofa once (I must have been lying on the floor, I often am). It was his best novel – *I Served the King of England* – and I took it away, read it, and returned it the

---

[1] *Cotswolds Privies*, Mollie Harris and Sue Chapman, Chatto & Windus, 1984.

next week a changed man. As for another friend's book of 19th-century French daguerreotypes of ladies spanking each other's bottoms, I can't make up my mind whether or not I'm glad I found it. My friend insists to this day that it[2] was a present that he was too polite to refuse. But my friends are an untrustworthy bunch. Especially him.

All of these – the rural privies, the Czech waiters, and the red-bottomed Frenchwomen – were chance encounters with Mr Rumsfeld, or, more precisely, with his idea of the unknown unknown. I would never have known to look for them. If I had been sitting at my computer, I wouldn't have *known* to search for them. I had to go outside. I had to let the element of chance in.

Computers are machines. The internet is, ultimately, a huge army of machines. And machines do not allow in the element of chance. They do exactly what you tell them to do. So the internet means that, though you get what you *already knew* you wanted, you'll never get anything more.

---

[2] *Jeux Des Dames Cruelles*, Serge Nazarieff, Taschen, 2000, since you ask.

THE GOOD BOOKSHOP

Yet such encounters are rare in the normal course of life, and we can't spend all day peering under sofas. And thus and therefore the Good Bookshop. Not the warehouse, not the internet, but the Good Bookshop. It is a room (or two) where the unknown unknowns of the world are laid out on tables and stacked in shelves. It is a room (or two) where you can find what you never knew you wanted, where your desires can be perpetually expanded. Not satisfied, because what point is there in satisfying a desire you already have? You are no better, no larger, at the end of it. A desire satisfied is a meagre and measly thing. But a new desire!

I'd never been a sci-fi sort of chap. I don't know why. I'd just never really bothered. I mean, I like science and I like fiction. I'd just not put the two together. So I don't know why I picked up a Philip K. Dick novel one day. The only explanation is that it was out on a table in a bookshop. I liked the first page. I liked the second page. And by the time I'd got to about page ten, I realised that the only decent thing to do was to buy it. When I finished it, I wanted more. Desperately. Luckily Dick wrote almost as fast as I read:

44 novels and fourteen short story collections. All these years later, I'm still happily chewing through them.

I never had any desire to read Ukrainian crime-comedy until 2001. I was promenading around a bookshop in north London and I saw a book called *Death and the Penguin*. It was out on a table, not the first table when you come in the door (footballers' autobiographies), but the table a little way back where the good stuff is always hidden. I liked the title – the move from abstract noun to concrete – I liked the cover – a man with a gun sitting in a bath with a huge penguin. It wasn't until after I'd picked it up, read the first paragraph and determined to buy it, that I noticed that it had been signed by the author. There are times when you can't part with your money quick enough. You just want to hurl a ten pound note at the girl behind the counter as you sprint for the street and somewhere to sit down and read.

If there's one thing that I've learnt from my long hours in Good Bookshops, it's that you *can* judge a book by its cover. I bought *Choke* by Chuck Palahniuk simply because the cover (back then) had a picture of a fry-up on it, and I was feeling hungry. I bought all his other books the next week.

It is, incidentally, a favour that e-books have done for the Good Bookshop: they have made books beautiful again. A few years ago, book covers could be rather drab affairs: the title and the author's name printed over a stock photograph of something Vaguely Relevant. If you wanted to read it, you had to take it as it was. Whereas now, in these new and glorious days when the margins on physical[3] are that little bit higher than on the electrical alternative, publishers produce exquisite bindings. Bookshops haven't been this pretty for at least a century.

BIBLIOMANCY: THE FUTURE OF BOOKS

The other advantage of the physical, paper-and-ink book is that you can flick through it. You can glance at the beginning, the middle and the end. Just as you found the book by chance, you can find a page by chance, or a particular paragraph or line.

---

[3] The trade terms are *physical* and *electronic* to describe paper and e-book respectively. I would much prefer *physical* and *metaphysical*, but my campaign has gained little traction, so far.

There's always a strange feeling you get when you come across one particular line by chance. It feels somehow significant. That's irrational of course, but humans are irrational creatures. Even the sturdiest, most down-to-earth chap will turn pale if he opens a book at random and sees the words PREPARE TO MEET THY DEATH.

This feeling is so deeply entrenched in human nature that many cultures have a practice called bibliomancy, where you use books to predict the future. When an ancient Greek fellow wanted to know what the future held for him, he would take a copy of the *Iliad* and let it fall open at a random page. Then he would point at a line, read it out, and that would be his fate. This was the *Sortes Homericae*.

The Romans did the same thing with Virgil. They called it the *Sortes Virgilianae*. Medieval chaps would do it with the Bible and called it the *Sortes Sanctorum*. There's a story about St Francis of Assisi doing it. He had just decided to give up all of his possessions, but then wondered whether that included his books, of which he was inordinately fond. So he opened the Bible at random and found the line:

> Unto you it is given to know the mystery of the kingdom
> of God; but unto them that are without, all these things are
> done in parables.

And somehow he worked out from that that he wasn't
allowed books, and that he didn't need them anyway. That's
just where St Francis and I differ.

The Catholic Church later condemned bibliomancy,
or fortune-telling through books. But you can still do
it, so long as you have a bookcase. When the Victorian
poet Robert Browning got engaged to Elizabeth Barrett,
he decided to use bibliomancy to see whether the
relationship would work. So he went to his bookcase
and took a volume down without looking at the title.
Obviously, what he was looking for was a bit of encour-
agement. Reassurance from the mystical world of books.
Something to tell him that love would conquer all, that
sort of thing.

He was therefore rather annoyed to discover that
he'd picked a book on grammar. Italian grammar, to be
precise. So he did what any rational man would do, and
quickly lowered his standards. He decided that if he found

a conjunction that was a Good Omen, or maybe just a possessive pronoun.

He opened the book and, because it was on Italian grammar, there were translation exercises in there. The first line he saw was:

> If we love in the other world as we do in this, I shall love
> thee to eternity.

You can't do that with an e-book.

I still practise bibliomancy myself. I do it with P.G. Wodehouse, who seems to have had an unerring knowledge of the inner workings of my soul. I just tried it, and found the line 'I am a vapid and irreflective chump'.[4]

It pains me to say it, but bibliomancy works.

THE GHOST IN THE BOOKSHOP

Bibliomancy works (or seems to work) because we can't help but find God in random things. It's that moment of

---

[4] From *The Inferiority Complex of Old Sippy*.

discovery, in the back of the bookshop, when your hand pulls out some funny little tome, with a funny little cover and you say to yourself: 'Yes. This is what I'm going to read next.'

It doesn't matter what the book is. It's the one that caught your eye. Or perhaps it's just the one that caught your hand. But in a Good Bookshop that is good enough. In a Good Bookshop all the books are good.

Half of the art of bookselling is about choosing what *not* to have in your shop. It is not enough to have good books, you must not have bad books.

If a bookshop contained every book ever written, what are the chances that you would find the *one* book you need? Well, they'd be perfect if you *already knew* what you needed, but, as I have been saying, that is not the point of a bookshop. That's something for the internet. No, the perfect bookshop is small, small and selective.

You should be able to go in blindfolded, reach out your hand at random and find something wonderful. I mean, I'm not actually recommending that you go in to a bookshop blindfolded and try this. You'd probably knock something over. Or accidentally punch a bookseller in the face. But you see the principle? Small and perfectly stocked. One of my favourite places to buy books used to be a stall just off Hampstead High Street where about seven boxes were laid out. I wish I could have read every book they had. But they are no longer.

The ideal trip to the bookshop, the perfect, perfect, can-never-exist-in-this-world visit to a bookshop works like this. I find the shop down a narrow street in a town that I have never visited before. I go in, and there is only one book. Just one. It is laid out on a table in a plain cover. I cannot even see the title. I buy it, and it tells me all the secrets of the universe.

I know that can never happen, but it might make a good first chapter for a novel.

THE ROMANTIC BOOKSHOP

Romance is about not getting what you wanted. It is an absolute necessity of any good romantic story that, at the beginning, the two lovers have no interest in each other. In *Pride and Prejudice* Elizabeth Bennet takes an immediate dislike to Mr Darcy. And Mr Darcy despises Elizabeth

Bennet. She thinks he is rude, arrogant and taciturn. He 'scarcely allowed her to be pretty' and her manners were 'not those of the fashionable world'. It is only later that he realises 'the very great pleasure which a pair of fine eyes in the face of a pretty woman can bestow'. It is only much later, after she has *accidentally* discovered what an expensive house Mr Darcy owns, that Elizabeth starts to love him back.

It's the same with Romeo and Juliet. When the play opens Romeo is in love with some other girl called Rosaline and wants to be with her and her alone. Juliet isn't in love with anyone in particular, but she's certain of one thing: she hates the Montague family. It's only when they *accidentally* see each other at a masked ball that he realises that Rosaline's a dud; and Juliet exclaims:

My only love sprung from my only hate!
Too early seen unknown, and known too late!

Of course it all ends in tears and poison, but it's sure as Hell romantic.

Benedick and Beatrice, Henry Higgins and Eliza Doolittle, Rick and Ilsa. If you'd asked any of them in scene one what they wanted from life, the answer would be 'Anyone but them!' It's the basic formula of any romance. They never wanted it at first, but of all the gin-joints in all the towns in all the world, you *accidentally* walked into this one.

Or, for the purposes of this essay, of all the bookshops, in all the towns, in all the world, you *accidentally* walked into this one, and *accidentally* fell in love with this particular book.

And again, yet again, the internet has produced the pernicious possibility of getting what you wanted. Internet dating allows you to name the exact specifications of the man or woman that you wish to acquire. Height, weight, income, shoe-size, star sign, blood-type, allergies, favourite horror movie, inside-leg measurement, political leanings and preferred breakfast cereal. You can choose them all. You can set your parameters. And, if you do that, you will get what you *already knew you wanted*.

You won't get Mr Darcy. You won't get Miss Bennet. Romeo would have specified *NO CAPULETS* and Juliet would have specified *NO MONTAGUES*. In everything else Romeo and Juliet might have got together. Two noble families, both alike in dignity. She's thirteen, he's sixteen-ish. An algorithm could get them together. But the one thing that makes the relationship romantic would have stopped it happening via machine, via computer.

The modern *Romeo and Juliet* would have run like this. He hated Capulets. She hated Montagues. So they searched around on www.barelylegalveronesesingles.co.it and both ended up reasonably, but not very, happy with people who matched, but did not change, their specifications.

Pride and Prejudice, in the internet age, would run:

> It is a truth universally acknowledged, that a single man in possession of a good fortune, must have already posted his details and requirements online and be working through the responses. Reader, I Googled him. THE END.

Of course, they all got what they wanted – the Darcys, the Benedicks, the Beatrices – but they got what they never knew they wanted. And that is what makes their stories romantic.

Lord, deliver us from what we *already knew we wanted*. Give us some new desires, the weirder the better.

THE THEOLOGY

There is an interesting and rather paradoxical idea in philosophy and theology that a chap can be enslaved by his desires. The idea is that your desires are something separate from you that boss you around. So hunger forces me to eat, thirst forces me to drink (that's my excuse), and curiosity forces me to kill a cat.

By this view, I will never find peace because I will always be running around trying to appease these unappeasable masters. That's why Buddhism asks you to free yourself from desire. That's why St Augustine said that the service of God is perfect freedom. My aims as a religious visionary are more modest.

I don't think I'm enslaved by my desires, largely because I'm not sure how I'd pass my time if I didn't have them. Take away my thirst, and I'd have a good fifteen hours a day with nothing to do. But I am sometimes *fenced in* by my desires. Because I already know what I like, I never try anything new.

I have my favourite morning walk, and my favourite pub, and my favourite restaurant. I have God-knows how many hours of my favourite music to listen to. I have my favourite whisky to drink as a nightcap. And my life is arranged in such a way that they are all within easy reach. Especially the whisky.

And so I never try anything else. To give you a small and heart-rending instance of this: I realised on Monday that I had never in my life drunk Dubonnet. Probably never will. I'm a whisky man, you see. Scotch. Islay malt for preference.

But … perhaps I'd like Dubonnet. You never know. It was on Monday that I realised that I'd never tried it. It's now Saturday. There is a shop precisely 258 yards from where I am now sitting that sells Dubonnet. I've been in there several times this week. But … but I am fenced in by my desires. I prefer my known knowns. I prefer getting the things that I already knew I wanted.

Bugger it. I'm off to buy some Dubonnet. I suggest you do too. When I return, we shall discuss geography.

GEOGRAPHY

'Now when I was a little chap I had a passion for maps. I would look for hours at South America, or Africa, or Australia, and lose myself in all the glories of exploration. At that time there were many blank spaces on the earth, and when I saw one that looked particularly inviting on a map (but they all look that) I would put my finger on it and say, "When I grow up I will go there." The North Pole was one of these places, I remember. Well, I haven't been there yet, and shall not try now. The glamour's off. Other places were scattered about the Equator, and in every sort of latitude all over the two hemispheres. I have been in some of them, and … well, we won't talk about that. But there was one yet – the biggest, the most blank, so to speak – that I had a hankering after.

'True, by this time it was not a blank space any more. It had got filled since my boyhood with rivers and lakes and names. It had ceased to be a blank space of delightful mystery – a white patch for a boy to dream gloriously over.'

Joseph Conrad, *Heart of Darkness*, 1899

These days he could use Google Earth. The known
unknowns, the blank spaces on Mr Conrad's map, have
all been filled in. Almost the last place to go was northern
Canada. It was after the Second World War, and there were
a lot of planes left over and a lot of qualified pilots and they
buzzed over the tundra, taking notes, taking photographs,
and taking away the fun of exploration for ever. That's when
we really got interested in other planets. They were all we
had left.

The known unknowns are few and far between. There
are a few left, of course: deep oceans, dark matter, why
animals sleep. Although I like to think that Mr Conrad
answered that one with those words 'dream gloriously'.

The glamour's off. Almost any question you ask can be
answered. It's only the questions that you didn't know to
ask that remain, dancing the can-can behind your back.
The unknown unknowns.

They're still there. They're everywhere. Juliet is still
waiting for you at the masked ball, if only you'll go along.
And she'll wait for you for ever. And the book is still waiting for you, the perfect book, the one that will answer
every question you didn't know to ask. It's on the shelf at

the top, in the corner, just within reach of your grasping hand. The unknown unknown, waiting like an undiscovered continent, just at the back of the bookshop.

That's what he was talking about, the great sage, the prophet, the messenger: Donald Henry Rumsfeld.

The message is that there are no 'knowns'. There are things we know that we know. There are known unknowns. That is to say there are things that we now know we don't know. But there are also unknown unknowns. There are things we do not know we don't know.

So when we do the best we can and we pull all this information together, and we then say well that's basically what we see as the situation, that is really only the known knowns and the known unknowns. And each year, we discover a few more of those unknown unknowns.

It sounds like a riddle. It isn't a riddle. It is a very serious, important matter.

Mark Forsyth,
Marciac, April 2014

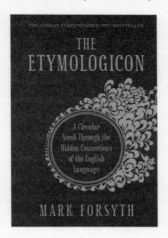

THE HOROLOGICON

A Day's Jaunt Through the Lost Words
of the English Language

'Magical ... a selection of those obsolete,
but oh-so-wonderful words' *Daily Mail*

The Horologicon – BBC Radio 4 *Book of the Week* – is an
entertaining guide to weird words for familiar situations, from
ante-jentacular to *snudge*.

£8.99 • Paperback • 272 pages • 978-184831-598-3

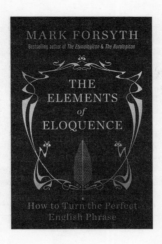

THE ELEMENTS OF ELOQUENCE
How to Turn the Perfect English Phrase

'An informative but highly entertaining journey through the figures of rhetoric … Mark Forsyth wears his considerable knowledge lightly. He also writes beautifully.' David Marsh, *Guardian*

The Elements of Eloquence divulges rhetorical tricks used by the Ancient Greeks and Katy Perry alike, demonstrating how phrases like 'Bond, James Bond' are effective because it's not what you say that's important, but how you say it.

£8.99 • Paperback • 224 pages • 978-184831-733-8

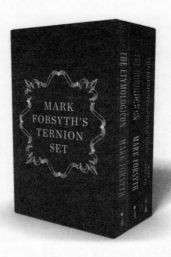

MARK FORSYTH'S TERNION SET

A beautiful box set containing *The Etymologicon*,
The Horologicon and *The Elements of Eloquence* in hardback.

£35 • Three hardbacks • 978-184831-738-3
• Published November 2014